Horses

Julie Murray

Abdo
FARM ANIMALS
Kids

abdopublishing.com

Published by Abdo Kids, a division of ABDO, PO Box 398166, Minneapolis, Minnesota 55439.
Copyright © 2016 by Abdo Consulting Group, Inc. International copyrights reserved in all countries.
No part of this book may be reproduced in any form without written permission from the publisher.

Printed in the United States of America, North Mankato, Minnesota.

052015

092015

Photo Credits: iStock, Shutterstock

Production Contributors: Teddy Borth, Jennie Forsberg, Grace Hansen

Design Contributors: Candice Keimig, Dorothy Toth

Library of Congress Control Number: 2014960328

Cataloging-in-Publication Data

Murray, Julie.
 Horses / Julie Murray.
  p. cm. -- (Farm animals)
ISBN 978-1-62970-941-3
Includes index.
1. Horses--Juvenile literature.   I. Title.
636.1--dc23
                    2014960328

Table of Contents

Horses

Horses live on farms.

Some horses are brown
or white. Others are black.
Some have spots or markings.

Horses have **manes**.

They also have long tails.

Girl horses are mares. Boys are stallions. Babies are foals.

mare

stallion

foal

11

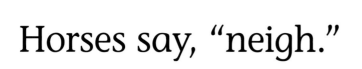

Horses say, "neigh."

Most horses sleep in a barn.

This keeps them warm and dry.

Horses eat hay, grass, and grain. They like apples and carrots too!

Some horses can be trained to ride. Gus rides a horse.

Have you seen horses on
a farm?

A Horse's Life

drink water

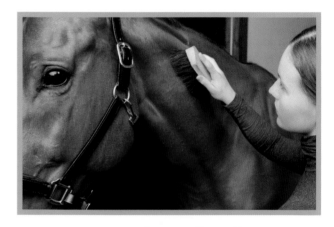

get brushed

eat hay

give rides

Glossary

mane
the long hair on the neck of a horse.

marking
a mark or repeated mark on an animal's fur or skin.

Index

abdokids.com

Use this code to log on to abdokids.com and access crafts, games, videos, and more!

Abdo Kids Code:
FHK9413